A CASE FOR HOSPITALITY

A Case For Hospitality

Chyina Powell

Published by Chyina Powell, 2024.

A CASE FOR HOSPITALITY

First edition. January 3, 2024.

Copyright © 2024 Chyina Powell.

ISBN: 978-1736463123

Written by Chyina Powell.

Also by Chyina Powell

Nevertheless: What The Bible Says About Mental Health
A Case For Hospitality

Watch for more at https://www.powelleditorial.org.

.

Table of Contents

To the ones who remind me how to be kind even when life is hard.

CHAPTER ONE
Introduction

What is hospitality? Most of the time, a person today would think of hotel management or something like that. But as Christians, follower of the resurrected King, we should know that isn't the case. Sometimes words lose their meaning over the years, sometimes meanings change (this is called semantic change). But fellow followers of Christ, we are tasked with being hospitable, and I'll give you exact verses later on, so it is imperative that we know what it means to be hospitable.

Firstly, I want to point out to you that Christian hospitality is not like worldly hospitality or even entertaining guests.

In this short book, we will cover quite a lot but not nearly enough. Together we will cover:

- What Christian hospitality is and is not,
- Some reasons hospitality is a dying art,
- Why we ought to be hospitable,
- And whom we are to be hospitable to.

All throughout, I will use scripture as a basis for what I share. Why? So that you can read it, look it up for yourself and realize that I am not making any of this up. The Lord wants our souls to prosper and one way we do that is by learning to live how he desires us and then doing it! (We cannot, ought not, learn just for the sake of knowing. To know to do good and not is sin, after all [James 4:17].) My scripture references will come out of the King James Version (KJV) unless otherwise marked. However, if you are more comfortable using another version of Scripture, please use the version that Holy Spirit has led you to use.

My prayer is that this book would not just enlighten you but also encourage you to act. And that in doing so, you inspire others to do likewise because in being hospitable you are showing Kingdom to the world. For those who take notes, if you have the physical version, you will see a couple pages for notes at the end of this book (feel free to use the margins as well.) And for those e-readers, please post your thoughts in your Notes app or whatever method your prefer!

Moreover, I hope that you will not only work on being hospitable but that you will also accept hospitality with a grateful heart.

CHAPTER TWO

What Is Hospitality?

N ow that I've posed the question, I hope you're in the mood for listening! According to the Oxford dictionary, hospitality is "the friendly and generous reception and entertainment of guests, visitors, or strangers." But it can also be the business of "providing food, drink, and accommodation for customers of restaurants, bars, etc. or guests at hotels." And in fact, that is how most people use it. But the truth is that when a Christian thinks about hospitality, that is not the way he or she should define it. The Bible gives us various examples of individuals showing hospitality and even warns us to be careful because we don't know who we might be entertaining (Hebrews 13:2). So, what is Christian hospitality? Firstly, I urge you to take a few seconds to think of what hospitality means to you, write it down if you so choose.

Let's go into it together. Christian hospitality, in short, is showing the love and grace of God to those around you. Christian hospitality can be done in numerous ways, and we will get to that later, and this is an oversimplified definition to be sure, but it's one that is easy to remember and I pray that as you read through the scriptures that I present, you will gain a deeper understanding of hospitality. In fact, I pray that the Lord via His Holy Spirit will open your mind to understand the text and give you deeper understanding because as His children, we are called to know the mysteries of God (Luke 8:10)!

In the Old Testament and even after Jesus ascended into Heaven, hospitality was hugely important. How you treated your guests was a reflection on your personal character. Treating your guests or any strangers that came into your home in an unbecoming manner would have been unthinkable at the time. Even wealthy home owners treated strangers with care and kindness. It was just the standard way of doing things. That was the culture at the time and even important people cared tremendously about treating their guests with honor and dignity. (We too, must treat others in such a manner.)

For an example, let's take a look at Lot. We know him as Abraham's nephew, we remember how he escaped Sodom and Gomorrah, we know about his wife turning into salt. All of that is great but I want to focus on how he welcomed his guests. Let me give you some background into Genesis 19. I won't place the entire passage here, but I highly suggest you read it.

Two angels (posing as regular men) came to Lot while he was sitting in the city gate. In that day and age, only extremely important people were allowed that position. They had to be of good moral fiber and they also carried various responsibilities in the city. Typically, political or religious leaders sat in the gate. Lot wasn't a nobody in Sodom. These angels find him and Lot immediately invites them into his home to wash their feet and rest, yet the angels said they would stay in the street. However, the Bible tells us that Lot "pressed upon them greatly" meaning he practically begged them to allow him to serve them and they agreed and entered his house where he prepared a meal (Genesis 19:1-3). I don't know about you, but I have never begged anyone to let me serve them nor begged a stranger to come stay in my home. As I said, Lot wasn't a nobody! He could have just as easily paid for them a room in an inn somewhere, but no. He made sure they ate and bathed and were welcomed. He was on a mission to serve! Isn't that interesting?

Where In The Bible Does It Talk About Hospitality?

FIRST, I WANT TO CLEAR up any confusion or misconceptions that you may have on whether or not we truly are called to be hospitable. Below, I will place some passages of scripture, feel free to read them here or in whatever version you prefer. Then take some time to highlight or underline or mark up in whatever way you see fit, clear examples of hospitality.

Let's look at Isaiah 58 6-10:

^{6}Is not this the fast that I have chosen? to loose the bands of wickedness, to undo the heavy burdens, and to let the oppressed go free, and that ye break every yoke?

^{7}Is it not to deal thy bread to the hungry, and that thou bring the poor that are cast out to thy house? when thou seest the naked, that thou cover him; and that thou hide not thyself from thine own flesh?

^{8}Then shall thy light break forth as the morning, and thine health shall spring forth speedily: and thy righteousness shall go before thee; the glory of the Lord shall be thy reward.

^{9}Then shalt thou call, and the Lord shall answer; thou shalt cry, and he shall say, Here I am. If thou take away from the midst of thee the yoke, the putting forth of the finger, and speaking vanity;

^{10}And if thou draw out thy soul to the hungry, and satisfy the afflicted soul; then shall thy light rise in obscurity, and thy darkness be as the noon day:

James 2:14-17 (English Standard Version aka ESV)

[14]What good is it, my brothers, if someone says he has faith but does not have works? Can that faith save him? [15]If a brother or sister is poorly clothed and lacking in daily food, [16]and one of you says to them, "Go in peace, be warmed and filled," without giving them the things needed for the body, what good is that? [17]So also faith by itself, if it does not have works, is dead.

Deuteronomy 24:19-22 (ESV)

[19]"When you reap your harvest in your field and forget a sheaf in the field, you shall not go back to get it. It shall be for the sojourner, the fatherless, and the widow, that the Lord your God may bless you in all the work of your hands. [20]When you beat your olive trees, you shall not go over them again. It shall be for the sojourner, the fatherless, and the widow. [21]When you gather the grapes of your vineyard, you shall not strip it afterward. It shall be for the sojourner, the fatherless, and the widow. [22]You shall remember that you were a slave in the land of Egypt; therefore I command you to do this.

Deuteronomy 15:11

[11]For the poor shall never cease out of the land: therefore I command thee, saying, Thou shalt open thine hand wide unto thy brother, to thy poor, and to thy needy, in thy land.

Doesn't this sound like hospitality to you? Giving food to the hungry? Bringing in those without homes? Clothing those who cannot clothe themselves? And these are just a few examples! This isn't something I made up just so I had content to write this book, it is real and the evidence is right there in your Word! I highly encourage you to take some time to read up on similar scriptures, as the Word says we have to study to show *ourselves* approved (2 Timothy 2:15). No matter what I place in this short book, there's always work for you to do. And as Christians, we enjoy getting to know our Father better, so maybe pick up a concordance or Bible dictionary, or simply search online and learn more about what the Father is trying to share with you today and everyday.

Let's look at one more example of hospitality: Abraham. In Genesis 18:2-5, Abraham is sitting at the door to his tent when he looks up and sees three men. Abraham, the patriarch of all Israel, runs out to greet these strangers and then he bows to them. That's right, he bows. You can read the rest of what he does for yourself, I just want to point out that there is a Biblical precedent, it is nothing new!

The Bible does not stop at mentioning hospitality, even in the verses above, you can see that we are called to be hospitable time and time again, to be caring and affectionate toward others. The scriptures even give us a few ways that we can be hospitable. But how does that translate to our day and age? Let's take a look at some ways that you can be hospitable in today's culture since most of us don't have fields to allow others to glean from after all!

What are some ways that we can be hospitable?

YOU, HOPEFULLY, HAVE a basis as to what hospitality is, so let's consider some of the ways that one can be hospitable. In the Old Testament, hospitality most commonly looked like opening up your home to the man or woman of God, feeding them or giving them money so that they could continue on without worry of their provision. For example, let's take a look at 2 Kings 4:9-17.

⁹And she said unto her husband, Behold now, I perceive that this is an holy man of God, which passeth by us continually.

¹⁰Let us make a little chamber, I pray thee, on the wall; and let us set for him there a bed, and a table, and a stool, and a candlestick: and it shall be, when he cometh to us, that he shall turn in thither.

¹¹And it fell on a day, that he came thither, and he turned into the chamber, and lay there.

¹²And he said to Gehazi his servant, Call this Shunammite. And when he had called her, she stood before him.

¹³And he said unto him, Say now unto her, Behold, thou hast been careful for us with all this care; what is to be done for thee? wouldest thou be spoken for to the king, or to the captain of the host? And she answered, I dwell among mine own people.

¹⁴And he said, What then is to be done for her? And Gehazi answered, Verily she hath no child, and her husband is old.

¹⁵And he said, Call her. And when he had called her, she stood in the door.

¹⁶And he said, About this season, according to the time of life, thou shalt embrace a son. And she said, Nay, my lord, thou man of God, do not lie unto thine handmaid.

[17]And the woman conceived, and bare a son at that season
that Elisha had said unto her, according to the time of life.

A Shunamite woman had taken notice of how the prophet Elisha
often spent time in her city and felt that it would be nice if he had a
place where he knew he would be welcomed. She then asks her husband
for permission and so they build Elisha a room and furnish it for him.
There are two things that I wish to draw your attention to here: the fact
that the Shunamite woman had no ulterior motives, she just wanted to
be of service to the prophet; and that because of her willing hospitality
she was blessed (a woman who believed she could not have children bore
a son). As a side note, if you ever want to look into people of great faith
in the Bible, continue reading the Shunamite woman's story, it is truly
interesting. But we are not here to focus on that aspect of her life, but on
her willingness to be hospitable.

The Bible reminds us that the Lord looks at the heart time and time
again, and our attitude and motives play a big part in our outcome (1
Samuel 16:7, Jeremiah 17:10, Proverbs 21:2). Just because we are doing
something good does not mean that we will be blessed if we are doing it
for the wrong reasons. We cannot manipulate God into blessing us and if
we want acclaim or praises by others for our good deeds, that is all we will
get (Matthew 6:1). The woman in the passage of scripture above had no
ulterior motives, it hadn't even crossed her mind that the prophet might
do something for her in return, she just wanted to be a blessing. This is
the mindset that all of God's children ought to have. We should want to
be a blessing simply because it is what God asks of us. However, when we
are obedient to the will of God (and it *is* His will that we are hospitable)
we are blessed because that is one of many promises. And our Father does
not go against His word.

In this text, the woman went above and beyond. I am not saying that
you should all go and build additions to your homes. But I want to point

out how her heart was postured for hospitality. She was just that willing
to do something to help someone else.

Here are some ways that we as believers can be hospitable:

- Donating Time
- Donating Money
- Providing A Listening Ear
- Providing Food
- Allowing Someone To Stay In Your Home

Most assume that the only way to be hospitable is to let someone in
your home, but I told you we were going to do some learning, didn't I?

Donating Time

IT MIGHT SOUND A BIT strange to use the word "donating" in
relation to time, but the truth is our time is limited and no one knows
how much time he or she has left in this life. So when you're giving your
time to someone or something that does not benefit you in any way, it is
almost like donating it, isn't it?

The truth is that not everyone has a home that can accept guests,
whether it be due to their lease, or they don't have room. But everyone
has time, whether they realize it or not. And when you donate time, you
allow people to see that you care for them, that you are concerned for
their wellbeing. It is our duty as representatives of Christ here on Earth
to show the world His love, and donating time is one way to do that.
We can donate time by volunteering at shelters and food banks. You can
even volunteer to babysit for a parent who has no way to afford childcare.
Maybe you can help read to children in your local library. All of these are
ways you can help show forth the love and compassion of our Lord and
Savior.

Think of some ways that you can donate your time and write them
down. Do it in the margin or on the Notes page. Perhaps list some of

the shelters near you that you can go to. There are shelters for battered women, rehab centers, shelters for the unhoused...the need is there, but as the Bible says, the laborers are few (Matthew 9:37).

Donating Money

THIS MAY SEEM OBVIOUS, but I will say it anyway. Donating money to the works of the Kingdom is always welcome. After all, it is up to the children of God to take care of the Lord's house and His workers. Think back to the Old Testament and the 12 tribes. Do you remember the Levites? The Levites were called by God to be priests and therefore, their inheritance looked a lot different than the inheritance of their kin. In fact, Deuteronomy 18:1 tells us that they have no inheritance or part with Israel. Because the Levites were dispersed among Israel, they had no land nor crops. They had to rely fully on what the children of Israel brought into the temple to sustain them. Don't believe me? Read Deuteronomy 18 in your spare time. And, as you know, the Bible bears witness of itself so there are many corresponding verses that help clarify that same point.

Likewise, when prophets were called, they had to leave their whole lives behind them. That meant no wealth or status or anything like that to get them into fancy hotels or get them the finest foods. No, that life was done. Look at the call of Elisha in 1 Kings 19:19-21. When Elijah thrust his mantel on his would-be apprentice, Elisha wanted to say goodbye to his parents, but Elijah said he could not. And then Elisha not only burns his plow but kills the oxen that were pulling it. Oxen were quite expensive in that day and Elisha's family had twelve teams of them. If they could afford 24 oxen, they weren't poor by any standards. Yet Elisha knew he had to give it up. Similarly, there are many teachers and preachers of God's Word who would not be able to make ends meet or do what God has tasked them with without the support of other believers. This is not me saying to donate to every tele-preacher or person who comes to your door, use wisdom and discernment. As the Spirit prompts, give what you can. And don't hold it over anyone's head that you gave. They don't owe you a favor, they haven't become your servant, nor do they owe you explanations for their actions here on out. Give without expecting to get anything back.

One great Biblical example would be the churches in Macedonia. Let's take a look at 2 Corinthians 8:1-5. This time I will be using the Contemporary English Version (CEV) not KJV:

> **8 My** friends, we want you to know that the churches in Macedonia have shown others God's gift of undeserved grace. ²Although they were going through hard times and were very poor, they were glad to give generously. ³They gave as much as they could afford and even more, simply because they wanted to. ⁴They even asked and begged us to let them have the joy of giving their money for God's people. ⁵And they did more than we had hoped. They gave themselves first to the Lord and then to us, just as God wanted them to do.

The churches in Macedonia saw a need and rose to meet it by giving financially to help the ministry. Verse two states that they were glad to give generously and the following verse states that they gave simply because they wanted to. No one twisted their arm in order to make them give. Have you ever heard the phrase, "The Lord loves a cheerful giver?" That is not just in giving tithes and offerings, but it in all our giving. Remember that whatever we do, we do unto the Lord so when you give, give with a cheerful heart (Colossians 3:23).

And if you are wondering about where to give, ask the Holy Spirit for guidance and look up some places in your area. Maybe consider some causes that mean a lot to you. Homelessness? Education? The safety of children? Safe drinking water? Accessibility? Missions trips? The Kingdom is moving in a lot of different ways so you are sure to find something that calls to you, just continue listening for His voice before you act.

Providing A Listening Ear

HAVE YOU EVER BEEN in a place where you just wanted someone to talk to? You didn't necessarily need them to give you answers or make your problems go away, you just wanted someone to listen and hopefully understand your feelings about your situation? The same is true for most people.

But here's a key point: **listen first, listen second, listen third.** Don't just listen and wait to get your point across. Because in doing so you aren't truly listening in the first place, even if you are hearing the words that the other is speaking. As Proverbs 18:2 states (I am paraphrasing) that fools are always concerned with expressing their own opinions and take no pleasure in understanding. We, as children of the Most High are told not to be fools time and time again. So, my brother or sister reading this, don't be a fool. Please listen and listen with the intent to understand, not to prove someone wrong or give them your opinion. And don't cut them off either, as fools answer questions before they are asked (Proverbs 18:13). How can you know the full extent of what that person is saying if you refuse to hear them out completely? Just by listening to another person wholeheartedly, you can encourage them. Did you know that?

Hospitality can be as simple as replenishing the spirit of another with encouragement, love and a helpful attitude. Don't make it harder than it has to be. A smile and an attentive ear goes a very long way!

Who are some people in your life that you can listen to? How would things in your own life be different if you would have had an attentive and listening ear in your hard moments? Think about that, maybe journal and jot some things down. Writing helps us remember and when you look back over your life, it causes you to be more grateful for what God has done in your life.

Providing Food

SADLY, WE LIVE IN A world where food is expensive. While the Lord gave us all we needed, not everyone has the means to get it. People around the world are dying daily simply because of poor food distribution and unhealthy or from the spoiled foods that they do consume. It is truly a sad state of affairs. While I am sure that you pray for the hungry and say grace over your meals, we aren't just called to pray, we are called to act. We are each given the responsibility to do what is within our means and so if you can provide a meal, consider doing so.

A hot meal on a cold day can do a lot more than most people think. You don't always have to go to a soup kitchen or a food pantry to provide food. You can make bagged lunches to pass out or even invite a visiting minister or family into your home for a meal and a warm heartfelt conversation. Or maybe you can take some groceries to someone you know who needs it. If your church has a Thanksgiving or Christmas giveaway, be sure to add a few names to the list when there's someone in your sphere of influence who is struggling.

Like the widow in Zarephath, don't be stingy give what you can (1 Kings 17:7-16).

If you're reading this, you may be asking yourself, "what if that person doesn't receive it?" That's okay too. You're job isn't to make them receive it is to open the invitation. Some may feel embarrassed to let others know they need food, and some may accept the food and still be upset with you. Trust me, I've had that happen.

In college, a friend of a friend was struggling as were his parents. All three were unhoused, living in their cars. I wanted to do something, and while I couldn't afford to do much as a college student trying to make ends meet, I did offer them a meal. I invited them over, they ate and the conversation was friendly and lighthearted. I hope that it took their minds off of some of the issues they were going through. And I know how nice a home-cooked meal can make you feel after getting by with fast food for so long. Later, when I was needing some encouragement, this person reached out to me. Perhaps after hearing my situation. And to put it lightly, they tore me down. They disregarded my emotions and told me my situation was my fault for a myriad of reasons. I am saying this to let you know that yes, there may be times when you show compassion and receive hostility. But I implore you, please don't let it stop you from being kind and caring to the next person. Maybe a warm meal will do more than fill their belly, maybe it will spark a hunger for the Lord, a hunger for change.

Think of a way that you, yes you, personally can provide food to someone in need.

Opening Up Your Home

THE LAST WAY THAT I wish to discuss for the purposes of this book is allowing someone to stay in your home. I saved this one for last because while it is often the first thing people think of when they hear the word "hospitality" it is usually the one that people are less inclined to actually do. (But I'll get into that in the next chapter.) We've seen how the Lord tells us to take in those who have been cast out of their homes and we saw how the Shunnamite woman welcomed the prophet Elisha into her home, even building a room just for him, but does the Bible give more examples? Of course it does!

There are many cases in the New Testament in which saints opened their house not only as a place to stay but as a place of worship. Here are a few examples:

1 Corinthians 16:19

[19]The churches of Asia salute you. Aquila and Priscilla salute you much in the Lord, with the church that is in their house.

Colossians 4:15

[15]Salute the brethren which are in Laodicea, and Nymphas, and the church which is in his house.

Acts 2:46

[46]And they, continuing daily with one accord in the temple, and breaking bread from house to house, did eat their meat with gladness and singleness of heart,

As you can see from this final verse, taken from the book of Acts, various saints opened up their homes, enough for people to fellowship and worship together, going from house to house with gladness because they were with one accord.

Again, opening up your home doesn't just mean allowing someone to stay! Opening up your home can also mean opening up your home for fellowship, a kind word or chat or get together. Let's take a look at Philemon.

[4]I thank my God, making mention of thee always in my prayers,

[5]Hearing of thy love and faith, which thou hast toward the Lord Jesus, and toward all saints;

[6]That the communication of thy faith may become effectual by the acknowledging of every good thing which is in you in Christ Jesus.

[7]For we have great joy and consolation in thy love, because the bowels of the saints are refreshed by thee, brother.

In Philemon verses 4 through 7, we see Paul showing his gratitude to the man for his reputation had reached Paul's ears. He had a reputation of showing love and his faith was well known. The Bible tells us that he "restored the saints." Love and generosity go along way when it comes to answering the Lord's call for hospitality.

What are some things you can take away from this chapter? Take a moment to jot them down? Do you feel as though you've learned more about what hospitality is and ways you can show it?

CHAPTER THREE

Why Is Hospitality Not A Thing?

H ospitality was so important hundreds of years ago, but it has died off. Why do you think that is? Take some time and write out a few reasons.

There are numerous reasons why hospitality isn't valued today, but here are a few that I want to list before we do a deeper discussion.

- Undervalued in Our Culture
- Pride
- Fear
- The Belief That Hospitality Was For "Then," Not "Now"

Did any of these make it into your list? Now that you are reading them, can you see where I am coming from? Let's take a deeper look into these four categories. And, just to warn you in advance, I really want to spend some time on the "fear" aspect of things. You may not agree, but I want to remove the masks that fear often wears when it comes to doing what God has called us to do.

Hospitality Is Undervalued In Our Culture

AS I MENTIONED, IN the Old Testament, hospitality was second nature. No one had to ask or remind someone to be hospitable, and if they did chances were they weren't going to stay in that person's house anyway. (Nobody wants to go somewhere they aren't wanted!) But it is highly undervalued today.

Hospitality is about making others feel comfortable and at home. When showing hospitality we are to be friendly, generous and eager! But that doesn't really align with societal standards does it? At least, I will say, in western culture. You hear people say that they have to take care of themselves or that they need to "secure the bag." The world looks at life and says "every man for himself" and hospitality, as with everything godly, it is direct opposition to the teachings and methods of the world. Hospitality tells us to treat everyone like family, to care for each other and share each other's burdens (Galatians 6:2). Yet, we live in the world. And our schools, jobs, colleagues and sometimes the dissatisfying circumstances we encounter lead us to believe that we are an island. It doesn't matter what is going on over there as long as me and my family are all right.

Let's take a look at Deuteronomy 5:7-11:

7If there be among you a poor man of one of thy brethren within any of thy gates in thy land which the Lord thy God giveth thee, thou shalt not harden thine heart, nor shut thine hand from thy poor brother:

8But thou shalt open thine hand wide unto him, and shalt surely lend him sufficient for his need, in that which he wanteth.

9Beware that there be not a thought in thy wicked heart, saying, The seventh year, the year of release, is at hand; and thine eye be evil against thy poor brother, and thou givest him nought; and he cry unto the Lord against thee, and it be sin unto thee.

[10]Thou shalt surely give him, and thine heart shall not be grieved when thou givest unto him: because that for this thing the Lord thy God shall bless thee in all thy works, and in all that thou puttest thine hand unto.

[11]For the poor shall never cease out of the land: therefore I command thee, saying, Thou shalt open thine hand wide unto thy brother, to thy poor, and to thy needy, in thy land.

As you can see, this verse tells us that we are to help the poor and not harden our hearts against them. To harden one's heart means to stubbornly ignore something. We cannot turn away from the poor, instead we are called to open our hands up wide to them. Likewise Proverbs 21:26 states that the righteous "give and spare not," meaning that they give what they can afford to give and don't hold anything back.

The reason that hospitality isn't popular is because there's nothing it for the person being hospitable, at least not from a worldly perspective. It's complete selflessness!

Everything pushes us against what scripture tells us to do and if we aren't guarding our hearts diligently, if we aren't monitoring what we listen to and what we see, we can fall victim to the lie that others don't matter. Maybe it comes in a more subtle way than that, oftentimes it does, but at the end of the day, when the curtain is pulled back, that's the truth that we have to face.

Have you ever thought about how society and your culture looks at hospitality? Is it valued? Is it something ignored and not talked about?

Pride

PRIDE IS A BIG ISSUE, even among Christians. And while we are all maturing in Christ, there are some things we still have to work on. In the case of hospitality, pride can masquerade as all sorts of things. Here are a few:

- I'm too busy for that. When would I have time to volunteer?
- I donate once a year to XYZ foundation, that's enough.
- Nobody helped me, they shouldn't be looking for handouts.

Can you think of a few more? I'm quite sure you can. Maybe you have heard someone say something along these lines or maybe you have said it yourself. Either way, that is a haughty spirit. And what does the Bible say about pride? Well Proverbs 18:12 says this:

12Before destruction the heart of man is haughty, and before honour is humility.

Pride leads to destruction. Being too proud to help another person will only harm you in the end. Let's look at a few other scriptures on pride.

Proverbs 16:18

18Pride goeth before destruction, and an haughty spirit before a fall.

Proverbs 16:5

5Every one that is proud in heart is an abomination to the Lord: though hand join in hand, he shall not be unpunished.

Jeremiah 13:15

15Hear ye, and give ear; be not proud: for the Lord hath spoken.

Romans 12:16

16Be of the same mind one toward another. Mind not high things, but condescend to men of low estate. Be not wise in your own conceits.

As always, if you are having trouble understanding the King James, feel free to use the version of scripture you are familiar with.

Are you beginning to see a pattern here? Pride doesn't lead to anything good, moreover, we are told to not be proud. There are hundreds of verses of scripture with similar meaning. And the Lord doesn't do anything without a reason, these scriptures are there because they are important. We cannot allow pride to cause us to be disobedient to the Lord's call for hospitality.

If you've had similar thoughts to the ones I placed above, have you ever considered why you are thinking that way? Have you ever considered what God feels about such thoughts? Maybe you have but you just don't know how to combat them. Maybe they feel like second nature because of how you were raised or your life's situations.

Together, I want us to take a look at the idea that needing help is the same as asking for handouts. Perhaps it is true that you were able to "pull yourself up by your bootstraps" but how can someone who doesn't have any boots accomplish the same thing? Also, since you were in a hard situation, you know how the struggle is, you know what it is like. Wouldn't it have been a relief, a breath of fresh air to have someone extend a hand toward you and help you out, even in a small way? Why wouldn't you want to do that for others? (That isn't a rhetorical question, I truly want you to think about it and maybe journal on it.) Scriptures tell us to be helpers one to another, to comfort and edify each other (1 Thessalonians 5:11). Your wisdom and insight from your experience can do both. Maybe you went through it so that you could help someone else get through it. Has that crossed your mind?

Pride is serious and, like in this example, pride can cause you to be disobedient to God, which as a believer is something I hope you never strive to do.

Fear

JUST LIKE PRIDE CAN wear many masks, so can fear.

Has there ever been a time in your life where you were afraid to do something the Lord tasked you with? Maybe it was just uncertainty, you didn't know if you were hearing correctly. Or maybe you felt like you should hold off, surely you could do it anytime, it didn't have to be right then. Well, that's a spirit of fear and what does 2 Timothy 1:7 tell us?

For God hath not given us the spirit of fear; but of power, and of love, and of a sound mind.

Perhaps you are wondering, but what if the person I am ministering (via hospitality) to doesn't like what I have to say? Guess what? That isn't on you, you do what you can do and let the Lord take care of the rest. Maybe you are thinking that the person you will let stay in your home may steal your valuables. Hide them. Lock your doors. If you know that person has such tendencies, use wisdom but don't let it keep you from obeying the commands of the Most High.

Fear is an emotion and while our emotions are always valid, they are not always real. What does this mean? God gave you emotions and they are good, they can do a lot of good. However, emotions are based on circumstances. Emotions cannot see the full picture. It's like trying to tell what a puzzle is when you only have one piece. We cannot let our emotions control our actions, especially not fear. Fear can keep us from walking in purpose. Fear can cause you to miss blessings and opportunities too.

Has fear ever kept you from doing something? What were the repercussions? How did that make you feel at the end of the day? Is that something you'd be willing to do again when you know that the promise is waiting for you? It's right there if you just do what God has tasked you with.

The Belief That Hospitality Isn't For Us Today

SOMETIMES, WHEN THINGS are old or seen as traditional, the world tells us to put them away. And sometimes we internalize that and carry it into our beliefs as Christians. While it is true that there are a lot of things that were done in the Old Testament that we no longer have to do, that doesn't mean that just because it was written back then means it has no relevance for us today. For example, we don't have to sacrifice lambs and oxen and turtledoves anymore because of Christ, but we *do* have to sacrifice ourselves daily (Romans 12:1-3). And just as back then, the Lord called for an acceptable sacrifice, He calls us to be acceptable sacrifices.

Galatians 3:24-27 tell us that the Old Testament is the schoolmaster to the new. And we, right now, are still living in the New Testament. That means, we are to learn from the Old Testament. Did you know that the New Testament didn't start until after Jesus died? So, if someone claims that the Old Testament isn't relevant, they are claiming that the teaching of Jesus Christ aren't relevant! Matthew 5 says this:

17Think not that I am come to destroy the law, or the prophets: I am not come to destroy, but to fulfil.

18For verily I say unto you, Till heaven and earth pass, one jot or one tittle shall in no wise pass from the law, till all be fulfilled.

Christ came to fulfill the law, and He wants us to remain in the law until the end. That means we have to line up with His Word and obey it. And since the Word calls us to hospitable, we should do it. It doesn't matter that it was written before you were born, it's still good. The Word of God still has meaning and if you want to see the goodness of the Lord while you live, it's best to be obedient.

We Can Triumph Over These Issues!

TRUE, THE WORLD WILL tell you that it isn't safe, that you don't have time. All of the reasons above and then some, but at the end of the day, who are you going to believe? Are you going to believe the Lord or the world? It may not seem that serious, but I tell you that it is. James 4:17 tells us "Therefore to him that knoweth to do good, and doeth it not, to him it is sin." You cannot claim to be ignorant now that you have read this far. Now that you know what hospitality is and that you should show it, failing to do so is counted as sin. And while the Father forgives, He does not want us abiding in sin. If the Lord tells you to do it, you have to make the choice to obey or disobey but those are the only two choices.

There is good news! We can overcome! In fact, we already have the victory since we are in Christ Jesus. Just as in the last chapter where I mentioned practical ways to be hospitable, I will list a few practical ways to triumph over the things that cause us to not want to be hospitable in the first place.

- Start small.

  ○ You don't have to start with big gestures. You can start with sharing kind words to those you encounter throughout the day and being personable and kind. Maybe instead of a full meal, you can bring someone a dessert or just a drink from the local cafe. By sharing small acts of kindness throughout the day, you are letting that person know you care and positioning yourself for more opportunities to share the love of God.

- Remember scripture.

○ When fear or pride comes, remember scripture. I highly suggest marking a few encouraging scriptures somewhere that you see frequently. Maybe you can make it the screen saver on your phone, maybe you can write it on a post it and put it on your work computer. However you choose to do it, be intentional about learning the Word.

• Pray.

○ Prayer is truly a gift from God. Think about it, He gives us a direct line to Him at all times of the day. We can't count on anyone the way that we can count on Him. I will go into this a little more later but pray that the Spirit will open your eyes to see the truth. Pray that you will have the courage to be kind to strangers, loved ones, ministers of the Word of God. Ask Holy Spirit how to do it. After all He is our Helper and our Teacher. We can go to Him when we need to. Then keep praying.

CHAPTER FOUR

Who We Should Be Hospitable To

We are coming closer to the end of our time together. I hope that you have gained some insight into hospitality and that you have considered ways you can be hospitable. I encourage you to also carry the wisdom you have gained and put it into action. Remember, there are many things out in the world trying to convince you not to be hospitable, but we have victory even over those things!

As you have read, we are called to be hospitable. Well, that is all well and good, but who are we to be hospitable to? Other believers? Everyone? Only those we like? Only those who look like they can give us something in return? Just as the Word tells us to be hospitable and why we ought to do so, it outlines whom we are to be hospitable to.

You may be thinking, "well isn't it the right thing to do to be hospitable to everyone?" That's a wonderful mindset to have, but the Bible actually says otherwise. That's right! There are some people that you should not be hospitable to. But before we get into that, let's look at those we *should* be hospitable to:

- Other believers
  ○ Especially those working in the ministry!
- Strangers
- Those who aren't saved

That's a small list but it encompasses quite a lot of people. You might have assumed that we ought to be hospitable to other believers and that is scripture-based. We are to show kindness to all believers, but it is imperative that we do our part to advance Kingdom work. Read Luke 10:1-8 and you'll see that Jesus is reminding the seventy disciples he is about to send out that the laborer is worthy of their hire. This means that those who work in the Kingdom deserve provision whether it be financially or through showing generous hospitality. (This is a bit of a tangent but this is why we should not fret over ministers and pastors and evangelists who receive wages, they work hard and deserve it!) This same sentiment is said again in 1 Timothy 5:18 and in 1 Corinthians 9:6-14. When you sow, expect to reap. That's a principle for life and it applies here as well.

Now, let's talk about strangers. I have mentioned this verse before but I want to highlight it again here, Hebrews 13:2.

Be not forgetful to entertain strangers: for thereby some have entertained angels unawares.

The Word of God tells us specifically not to forget to entertain strangers. This can mean a lot of things, but in short it means people you don't know. You shouldn't need another person's track record or background story to show them love and kindness or be a blessing to them. You should show the same amount of love and care to a stranger on the street that you do to a cherished friend or your brother or sister in Christ. Who knows? That person panhandling might be an angel in disguise.

Let me tell you a little story. I lived in Philadelphia during graduate school and one of my favorite grocery stores was Trader Joe's. It was maybe six or seven blocks from me, give or take a few. But city blocks aren't like the blocks in your everyday town and usually I took the trolley unless it was nice enough to walk. On this particular day, it wasn't and I had an umbrella (a nice Nautica one from my dad) and got on the trolley, got my groceries and came home. When I had put everything away, I realized I didn't have my umbrella. It had stopped raining by the time I got out of the store and so I hadn't even thought about it. Money was tight and that was the only umbrella I had with me so that meant I would have to go and get it.

On my second trip, there was a man sitting near the store. He had a cart with blankets and other things you might find on an unhoused person. This man asked me for money. Since I hadn't thought about it, I left home with no more than my trolley card and ID. I didn't have the money to give him. I told him, "I don't have any money but I can pray for you." And he said something along the lines of "That works. You can never have too much prayer." My thoughts exactly. So I prayed and he thanked me and then I went into the store to check out the lost and found. When I left the store, I'd been in for five minutes at most, the man and all his belongings were gone. There was no trace of him, like he had never been there. And it was a lot of stuff! I don't know if he was an angel or not, but I took the time out to talk and pray with him when others walked right by. I believe that is what's at the heart of Hebrews 13:2.

So who are the people we shouldn't be hospitable to then?

FALSE TEACHERS AND prophets. The Bible gives us many warnings against such individuals and let's us know that we shouldn't have anything to do with such people.

What is a false prophet?

A FALSE PROPHET, TO put it simply is someone who claims to speak on behalf of God but isn't or they have their own agenda. There are two types of false prophets I want to discuss with you today, those who hear the Word of God but then say something contradictory to it and those who don't hear anything from God but claim they do.

Let's look at the second type first. In Isaiah 13:2, the Lord through Isaiah says "Woe unto the foolish prophets, that follow their own spirit, and have seen nothing!" The very next verse compares such prophets to foxes. These are the kind of prophets who go without being sent by the Lord. They speak lies and the Lord says in Isaiah 13:10 that they seduce people away from truth. You probably wouldn't want someone else speaking for you who has no relationship with you, the same is true of God. He is not pleased when people claim to hear Him and have not and He is not pleased when such individuals lead His children astray, giving them false hope or causing them to fall prey to the enemy. I highly suggest you read all of Isaiah 13 when you have time as it gives a great picture into the harm these false prophets can cause.

There are some prophets who actually do hear from the Lord and yet don't bring forth the message that the Lord told them. Why is that? Maybe for pride or for financial gain. Maybe out of fear. Remember the prophet Micaiah was imprisoned multiple times because while he spoke the truth, it wasn't what the king wanted to hear (1 Kings 22). In fact, King Ahab accused Micaiah of lying to him since he only brought prophecies the king didn't want to hear. Actually, 1 Kings 22 is a great example of false prophets, so let's take a look, shall we?

⁵And Jehoshaphat said unto the king of Israel, Enquire, I pray thee, at the word of the Lord to day.

⁶Then the king of Israel gathered the prophets together, about four hundred men, and said unto them, Shall I go against Ramothgilead to battle, or shall I forbear? And they said, Go up; for the Lord shall deliver it into the hand of the king.

You read that right, 400 prophets lied to King Ahab and King Jehoshaphat. But that's not all.

[11]And Zedekiah the son of Chenaanah made him horns of iron: and he said, Thus saith the Lord, With these shalt thou push the Syrians, until thou have consumed them.

[12]And all the prophets prophesied so, saying, Go up to Ramothgilead, and prosper: for the Lord shall deliver it into the king's hand.

But after Micaiah gave his prophecy warning the kings not to go into battle and was thrown back in prison, the Lord chose to do something that you may not have thought He would do. The Lord called forth spirits to lie to Ahab and give the king false confidence to go into battle since he didn't want to believe the word of God. (But that is a whole other book!) I want to focus on how these spirits went into the same prophets that were lying anyway to make them double down on their claims that Ahab would be victorious. Isn't that something?

Are there other types of false prophets that you can recall from the scriptures? Take some time to think about it and jot them down.

What then is a false teacher?

A FALSE TEACHER, MUCH like a false prophet gives out misinformation and they lie for their own purposes. A teacher may make a mistake, but that doesn't mean they are a false teacher, it simply means they have more maturing to do in the Word. But when a person who is supposed to be teaching God's word intentionally perverts it, there's a problem there.

Before we get into a further discussion, take a look at 2 Peter 2:1-3

2 But there were false prophets also among the people, even as there shall be false teachers among you, who privily shall bring in damnable heresies, even denying the Lord that bought them, and bring upon themselves swift destruction.

²And many shall follow their pernicious ways; by reason of whom the way of truth shall be evil spoken of.

³And through covetousness shall they with feigned words make merchandise of you: whose judgment now of a long time lingereth not, and their damnation slumbereth not.

These false teachers are denying the Lord, bringing in heresies (beliefs contrary to the teachings of Christ) and many, *many,* shall follow them. And in verse two it tells us that eventually the truth shall be evil spoken of. Doesn't that sound like what is happening today? Where the good is becoming evil and evil is seen as good? We cannot forget verse 3! The NIV (New International Version) puts it like this:

³In their greed these teachers will exploit you with fabricated stories. Their condemnation has long been hanging over them, and their destruction has not been sleeping.

Because of their greed, false teachers are seeking to exploit the people of God. They want to use and abuse and mislead. It isn't on accident or by happenstance. And for this, they will be destroyed. No ifs, ands, or buts.

In 2 Corinthians 11:3-4, Paul warns us of being led astray from "sincere" and "pure devotion to Christ." You cannot be led astray by something that isn't tempting to you, so false teachers (and false prophets alike) often come with things that may sound good. Just as Ahab wanted to go to war so that is the prophecy he believed. Perhaps you like what this new teacher is saying, it sounds alright to you, so you get a little closer. Then you get a closer. And before you know it, you're out of relationship with God. And while you may be walking in a spirit, it is not the Holy Spirit. That is the goal of false teachers. True believers should NOT put up with it.

Where does it say to not show them hospitality?
LET'S TAKE A LOOK AT 2 John 10-11.

¹⁰If there come any unto you, and bring not this doctrine, receive him not into your house, neither bid him God speed:

¹¹For he that biddeth him God speed is partaker of his evil deeds.

This scripture tells us that if there is someone who is operating outside of the doctrine of Christ, we aren't to invite them into our homes or have anything to do with them or else it is like we are approving of what they are doing. The CEV (Contemporary English Version) puts it this way:

¹⁰ If people won't agree to this teaching, don't welcome them into your home or even greet them. ¹¹Greeting them is the same as taking part in their evil deeds.

To those who purposefully oppose God's Word and His teachings, we should have nothing to do with them! That is scriptural! In Ephesians 5:11, it tells us that we aren't to have fellowship with works of darkness. Don't you know that anything that is against God is darkness? Moreover, in Romans 16:17 it tells us to avoid those who cause division among the brethren. I mentioned before how one of the purposes of false prophets and teachers is to lead people away from the true and living God, didn't I? We are to avoid those who go against the doctrine of Christ. I highly encourage you to read these scriptures for yourself and meditate on them. It may seem harsh, avoiding people and having nothing to do with them as a Christian, but there is a purpose for all we do. As 1 Corinthians 10:21 tells us, we can't be partakers of the Lord's table and the table of devils. Either we are in or out in the Kingdom and when we begin to *condone* false teachers and prophets we make the choice to be out.

———— ⟨⟩ ————

For more reading on false prophets and false teachers:

- 1 Kings 13 (An older prophet lying to a younger one)
- Deuteronomy 13 (How to deal with false prophets)
- Acts 20:28-30 (Beware of those who draw away disciples)
- 1 Timothy 6:3-5 (Identifying false teachers)
- 1 John 4:2-3 (The spirit of antichrist)
- Gnosticism (A false teaching that was popular in the New Testament)

CHAPTER FIVE

When To Show Hospitality

So far, we've discussed what hospitality is, why it is important and whom we should be hospitable to. But we haven't really talked about when to show hospitality. The truth is, just like with prayer, you should be in a posture of graciousness and kindness at all times. And those two things are what lie at the heart of hospitality.

How To Get In The Posture Of Hospitality

IT IS MY OPINION THAT as lovers of the Lord and followers of Christ we should always be striving to be in the posture of hospitality.

The first step, as with most things, is to have the desire to be hospitable. And that desire should stem from the right motives. While God promises to bless us as we bless others (Proverbs 11:25, Philippians 2:3-4), that comes with some stipulation. Remember, our Heavenly Father looks at the heart and as Philippians 2:3 says, we can't do things just because we want to glorify ourselves. Likewise, we shouldn't be hypocritical, doing good things so that others will take notice of it and praise us. Maybe you don't naturally have the desire, that's okay because we are all different people and in different phases of life. Take a few moments to jot down a short prayer and ask God to help you, ask for a desire to be more gracious, to be humble and a desire to be willing to be hospitable.

The second step is to be vigilant. Just like in every other area of our lives, we have to be vigilant when it comes to our spiritual walk. The Lord gives us ample opportunities but we have to be sure not to squander them by letting them pass by. Ask the Holy Spirit to open your spiritual eyes so that you can see what the Lord is doing and recognize when He is giving you a chance to show grace and love to another person. Trust me, you may have to do this daily until you get in the habit of showing grace. And once you get into that habit, you'll see many more opportunities arise, you'll also begin to see the benefits of being a good representative of Christ.

The final step is to act. You can pray about it, you can even have your eyes open to notice when chances to be hospitable arise, but if you do not act all of that other stuff was in vain. You can make a habit of being prayerful but what does it say in James 1:22-25?

> ²²But be ye doers of the word, and not hearers only, deceiving your own selves.

> ²³For if any be a hearer of the word, and not a doer, he is like unto a man beholding his natural face in a glass:

> ²⁴For he beholdeth himself, and goeth his way, and straightway forgetteth what manner of man he was.

> ²⁵But whoso looketh into the perfect law of liberty, and continueth therein, he being not a forgetful hearer, but a doer of the work, this man shall be blessed in his deed.

We have to be doers of the Word! Hearing is the first step, but it cannot be the only step we ever take. Only those who do the Word will be blessed. Getting all the facts isn't enough, praying isn't enough. You have to go and live according to the Word. Take God up on those opportunities that you now begin to see. Trust me, He will help you as long as you are trying to do it. The Holy Spirit is our Helper after all.

So where do we go from here? Maybe we should take time out to think of some of the times we are called to be hospitable.

As A Form Of Gratitude

ONE PERSON THAT WE haven't talked about yet is Lydia. Lydia was a woman in the New Testament who heard the word of the disciples being preached and received God into her heart. Acts 16:11-15 tells us that Lydia was rather wealthy, she could sell purple cloth (a sign of nobility and royalty) after all. At the time in Philippi, there weren't enough men to establish a proper church (a law back then) and so since there was no formal meeting place, the people would often go to the riverbank to fellowship and pray. This is where Paul and his traveling companions met her.

> [14]And a certain woman named Lydia, a seller of purple, of the city of Thyatira, which worshipped God, heard us: whose heart the Lord opened, that she attended unto the things which were spoken of Paul.

> [15]And when she was baptized, and her household, she besought us, saying, If ye have judged me to be faithful to the Lord, come into my house, and abide there. And she constrained us.

Verse fifteen tells us that she was baptized and then brought her entire household (family and staff) to be baptized as well. And after she received the teachings of the apostles, she besought (begged) them to come stay in her house and they were constrained (persuaded) to do so. Lydia was truly grateful to the apostles for sharing the truth and wanted to show them that gratitude by opening up her home (which once again was the most common way to show hospitality in Biblical times).

Likewise, when we are grateful, we can show hospitality. Perhaps the message the pastor preached has given you new insight so you invite them and their family to a meal at your home. This is a perfect example of showing gratitude to a worker in the Kingdom!

As Holy Spirit Prompts

THOSE WHO HAVE THE Holy Spirit living within them know that He often tells us what to do, when to do it and how to do it. (Thank God for that!) When we listen to Him, He directs our paths and His direction brings joy without sorrow as well as many other benefits.

At times, Holy Spirit will bring someone to your mind or have someone in your path that could really use a kind word or a helping hand. Growing up, my mother used to say that when you woke up in the night with someone's face in your mind, that was a clue that you need to pray for that person. You don't need all the details, you just need to start praying. I believe the same can be true for hospitality. Have you ever been going about your day and then you think, "I wonder how so-and-so is doing?" Or maybe you're talking with someone else and they say, "Did you hear that this person had this happen?" That is a great chance, an open door to start a conversation and be a listening ear. Maybe this person does need a meal or a way to work or a safe place to stay for the night. But how will you ever know if you don't follow the prompting of the Spirit?

On another note, Holy Spirit paired with godly wisdom is a good indicator of when you should stretch out your hand to someone. After all, not everyone is open to receiving hospitality (they may call it handouts or charity). Plus, you don't always know what spirit that person is operating in and if you aren't wise, you may be putting yourself and others in danger.

What do I mean?

You can give anyone a meal or a ride to work, but you have to also guard your heart (Proverbs 4:23). The Lord will not put more on you than you can bear but you can. And while you are trying to do a good deed for someone else, they may be a burden you are not yet mature enough to handle. Your hear may be in the right place and that is **great** but you have to be wise! Wisdom isn't just knowing something. It is putting both knowledge and understanding into practice and using discernment as the Lord instructs. And if you are seeking wisdom, ask (James 1:5)! The Lord gives wisdom freely and abundantly after all. I don't want anyone to be cast away because they were seeking to do good and then they were led astray. That person who needs a ride to work may not look like they have a spirit of division on them but they do. They may claim to be walking after God, they may know scripture and pedagogy, but if they are trying to convince you of anything that is against the Word of God, they can be counted among those false teachers and spirits of antichrist we just finished talking about, even if they don't have that office.

This is the main reason that I urge you and all believers to study the Word for yourselves. How can you know a false teacher or false prophet or spirit of antichrist when you aren't reading, meditating on and studying your Word? Short answer? You can't. And you are liable to be led astray because you don't know any better. But the thing about it is, when you go, you're also liable to take others with you and that is not what God wants. So pray about it when you have to think on those "big" moments of hospitality like opening up your home or giving out your phone number for continued contact. At least until you are strong enough in the Lord and knowledgeable enough to discern the spirits that others are operating in and are able to withstand them. After all, in Ephesians 6:13-16, we are told that we put on the armor of God so that when it is all said and done, we are still standing. That was me paraphrasing, please don't quote that! But I will put Ephesians 6:13 here just for you!

Wherefore take unto you the whole armour of God, that ye may be able to withstand in the evil day, and having done all, to stand.

Believe me, the Lord loves the fact that you have the will to be of help to another, but that doesn't mean He wants you putting yourself at risk either physically or spiritually. Choose wisdom. Once you open yourself up to hear the Spirit of God, you'll be able to better determine when and to whom you should show hospitality to.

Do you feel that God has ever called you to be hospitable? Why or why not? When was it? Take some time to think back and write some ideas in the notes or in the margins.

CHAPTER SIX

On Receiving Hospitality

It's not always in our power to be hospitable. Sometimes, we are on the other side of things and we need someone to come along that is gracious enough and obedient to the Word of God to help us out.

How To Receive Hospitality

DID YOU KNOW THAT THERE is a right and a wrong way to receive the care of someone else? No? Well now you do. I mentioned this passage of scripture earlier in this book but let's circle back to it. Luke 10:1-9:

> **10** After these things the Lord appointed other seventy also, and sent them two and two before his face into every city and place, whither he himself would come.

> **2** Therefore said he unto them, The harvest truly is great, but the labourers are few: pray ye therefore the Lord of the harvest, that he would send forth labourers into his harvest.

> **3** Go your ways: behold, I send you forth as lambs among wolves.

⁴Carry neither purse, nor scrip, nor shoes: and salute no man by the way.

⁵And into whatsoever house ye enter, first say, Peace be to this house.

⁶And if the son of peace be there, your peace shall rest upon it: if not, it shall turn to you again.

⁷And in the same house remain, eating and drinking such things as they give: for the labourer is worthy of his hire. Go not from house to house.

⁸And into whatsoever city ye enter, and they receive you, eat such things as are set before you:

⁹And heal the sick that are therein, and say unto them, The kingdom of God is come nigh unto you.

I want to key in on verses seven and eight. The seventy disciples that had been sent out were sent into different cities with nothing but the clothes on their backs and had to rely on others for their needs to be met. But Jesus gives them specifics on what they are to do. When they find a house to stay, they are to stay there and eat and drink whatever their hosts bring to them. The Lord tells them specifically not to go from house to house. Why do you think that is? Take some time to write down your thoughts on the Notes page.

Here's the thing, Jesus didn't want the disciples to be ungrateful nor did he want hosts competing or feeling less than.

What do I mean by that? Think of it this way, you have a guest and you can afford to feed them chicken and they like it but then the very next day they decide to go over to Sister Susie's house or Brother

Johnny's house because they can afford steak. Now you've tidied your home, welcomed them in with a smile, but it wouldn't feel good if that guest did that. Maybe you would be hurt or angry. Maybe you would wonder if that guest didn't feel comfortable or if you were lacking or if you had done something wrong. That's all guilt isn't it? The Bible tells us that emotion is not of God.

And on the other side of things, a minister like in this case, has no right to choose whom he or she will fellowship with on the basis of what that person can do for them. Neither do we, fellow Christians. When we receive the generosity of someone else, receive it with gladness and a right spirit. It says right there in verse eight that we shouldn't be picky. Eat and drink what they give you, don't complain that they don't have cable or streaming services. So what if the WiFi is spotty? So what if the comforter is a little old and well-loved, isn't that better than sleeping out in the elements?

In the example above, by staying in one house, the disciples were showing their appreciation to that family. Moreover, it prevented division and disharmony among believers in that area (no one trying to compete against who could get the disciples to stay in their house the longest). And because the disciples weren't being picky or house-hopping, they had more than enough time to focus on the task at hand: spreading the teachings of Jesus.

This isn't just for the ministers or those who are working in the Kingdom full-time, this is for everyone.

Just as you have to have the right heart when you show generosity, you have to have that same heart and attitude when you receive it. What heart posture ought you to take when someone shows you kindness? Jot some things down. Take a minute or two to be real with yourself. Is that typically the way you think? Or are you someone who feels like you don't need anyone's help, that maybe they should mind their own business?

Brothers and sisters in Christ, we should never look down on someone who is trying to help. Nor should we think that we are too good to receive it. Who knows Holy Spirit might have placed you in someone's mind, maybe they just want to be a blessing to you. Don't be like a spoiled child complaining on Christmas morning because his gifts weren't exactly what he wanted. If you are struggling to purchase groceries (as most are in this economy) and a fellow believer brings you some, don't get upset because the brands on the labels aren't fancy or your first choice. Some food is better than no food.

Likewise, we should not turn down hospitality when someone offers it, unless it is the will of the Lord. (You can look at 1 Kings 13:1-29 for an example of when a man of God was told by God to not eat or drink in the town he was in.) Yes, the Lord sometimes tells you not to accept hospitality because it is for your benefit. However, if He has not specifically told you (and He always will if that is what He desires of you) than don't shun someone for trying to do a good deed. Don't mess up their blessing and yours. That's right, you can be blessed while on the other end of hospitality.

Maybe that person has a word from God just for you, but you won't answer their calls or keep making excuses when they mention grabbing a cup of coffee or tea. Maybe they know a way to help you pay off that credit card debt or a way to keep your house that is about to go into foreclosure, even though you haven't spoken a word about it to anyone. But just like a closed mouth doesn't get fed, closed ears don't hear. And when you fail to hear, you miss out on wisdom and age.

Why *choose* to do that?!

We should never choose to walk in darkness as we are children of the light. Who knows? That person may have been on the brink of giving up. They might have been sick of going out of their way for people and never getting a thank you, or feeling ignored. But you, by accepting help and being gracious enough to say a genuine "thanks" can change their perspective. Your gratitude and reception of the help they offer may be what motivates them to keep going, to keep being obedient to God, even when it looks like the reward is slow in coming. Have you ever thought about that?

The Lord's thoughts are much higher than our own and so there's a lot we will never understand, however, when He has made it plain for us, we should pay attention. 1 Thessalonians 5:18 tells us to be grateful in all things, therefore we should never shun someone's kindness.

> In every thing give thanks: for this is the will of God in Christ Jesus concerning you.

Have you ever shunned someone's kindness only to regret it later? What happened because of it? And have you ever had someone do it to you? How did it feel? For the next fifteen seconds, just think about it. You may have been trying to do a good deed, show someone you love them and are concerned for their wellbeing yet they go and turn their nose up at you.

How To React When Someone Doesn't Accept Hospitality

JUST AS YOU MAY HAVE done in the past, not everyone will be willing to receive hospitality. Whether they feel embarrassed or it is a matter of pride, they have their reasons for turning you down. In that case? What should your next course of action be?

Let's be real, when that happens, the first thing that often comes up is pride. Your thoughts may look something like this: "How dare they, I'm just trying to help." "They better not come asking me later, that's over and done with." "This is the last time I try to do something nice." "See, I knew I shouldn't have even tried." "Lord, help me because I have a few words and they aren't holy ones." "Man, whatever."

Trust me, there are a lot more. That's because when someone rejects something we are trying to give us flesh wants to make us think that the person is rejecting us. However, that's not the case. Plus, we can't let flesh have it's way *ever*. You may feel a bit heated, you may feel hurt, you may even be confused because you know for a fact this person or family is in need of help. But there is a right way to respond when someone rejects your showing of gracious hospitality. (I said gracious because hospitality shown begrudgingly isn't something we should be operating in.)

So what do we do?

- Take a breath. Calm down, remind yourself that you have done your part by offering, by extending the invitation.

- Smile. This shows that person that you aren't upset with them or hurt.

- Let them know you care. This can be done in all manner of ways. Maybe you offer to pray for them, or let them know they can call you when they want to talk.

- Walk away. It sounds strange to say "back down" but essentially, that's what we have to do. After all, you cannot force someone to accept your goodwill nor should you try to.

This process may take some getting used to, especially for those who aren't used to taking "no" for an answer. But it's worth it. Our job is to show love, not shove it down somebody's throat.

If you struggle with receiving hospitality or accepting it when someone turns you down, take some time to pray on it. Ask God to help you be humble and giving. Ask Him to give you peace when your kindness is "shot down" or rejected.

CHAPTER SEVEN

The Benefits Of Hospitality

I think that we have talked enough about this subject so I wish to leave you with a few truths to encourage you. As I've already mentioned, hospitality when done correctly, has numerous benefits. However, I think that it would be valuable to give you scriptural evidence that this is true.

Leviticus 25:35-26

35And if thy brother be waxen poor, and fallen in decay with thee; then thou shalt relieve him: yea, though he be a stranger, or a sojourner; that he may live with thee.

36Take thou no usury of him, or increase: but fear thy God; that thy brother may live with thee.

Luke 6:35

35But love ye your enemies, and do good, and lend, hoping for nothing again; and your reward shall be great, and ye shall be the children of the Highest: for he is kind unto the unthankful and to the evil.

What can we learn from these passages of scripture? That we are called to relieve a brother who is poor and exhausted, for one thing.

Moreover, when we are kind and do good (even to our enemies) God will rewards us. However, the trick is that we out not expect something in return from that person. Remember what I said about having the posture of hospitality? Well, this isn't a "give and take," "you scratch my back and I scratch yours" kind of lifestyle. Be hospitable to others even when you have absolutely *nothing* to gain out of doing so. And when you do, the Lord will bless you. After all, He is kind even to the evil, how much more kind will he be to the upright?

Need more evidence that a giving heart leads to blessing? Well, okay. Take a look at these verses and examples from scripture.

Psalm 112:5 (New King James Version)

> A good man deals graciously and lends;
> He will guide his affairs with discretion.

Proverbs 11:24-25

> [24]There is that scattereth, and yet increaseth; and there is that withholdeth more than is meet, but it tendeth to poverty.

> [25]The liberal soul shall be made fat: and he that watereth shall be watered also himself.

Proverbs 19:17

> [17]He that hath pity upon the poor lendeth unto the Lord; and that which he hath given will he pay him again.

Proverbs 21:13

> [13]Whoso stoppeth his ears at the cry of the poor, he also shall cry himself, but shall not be heard.

Proverbs 22:9

⁹He that hath a bountiful eye shall be blessed; for he giveth of his bread to the poor.

Luke 3:10-11

¹⁰And the people asked him, saying, What shall we do then?

¹¹He answereth and saith unto them, He that hath two coats, let him impart to him that hath none; and he that hath meat, let him do likewise.

Acts 20:35

³⁵I have shewed you all things, how that so labouring ye ought to support the weak, and to remember the words of the Lord Jesus, how he said, It is more blessed to give than to receive.

2 Corinthians 9: 6-11

⁶But this I say, He which soweth sparingly shall reap also sparingly; and he which soweth bountifully shall reap also bountifully.

⁷Every man according as he purposeth in his heart, so let him give; not grudgingly, or of necessity: for God loveth a cheerful giver.

⁸And God is able to make all grace abound toward you; that ye, always having all sufficiency in all things, may abound to every good work:

[9](As it is written, He hath dispersed abroad; he hath given to the poor: his righteousness remaineth for ever.

[10]Now he that ministereth seed to the sower both minister bread for your food, and multiply your seed sown, and increase the fruits of your righteousness;)

[11]Being enriched in every thing to all bountifulness, which causeth through us thanksgiving to God.

God promises us in 2 Corinthians 9:11 that when we give (which is a form of ministry if you were unaware) we will be bountifully enriched in everything. God won't just provide, He will fill your cup to overflowing! Isn't that amazing. What other scriptures come to your mind when you think of God's blessings overflowing in your life? Maybe you should write them down! That way you can look back at them and encourage yourself with the truth of the Word of God.

Not only will the Lord bless you when you show hospitality but by showing hospitality instead of turning away from those in need you are making sure that your prayers get to the ears of our Father instead of just bouncing off the walls and the ceiling of your home. And we all know that God answers every prayer He hears and many blessings come from answered prayers. Can you think of a time when you gave and were later blessed? Perhaps you never thought to make a connection between the two but when you sow, you reap. Take some time to think about a couple instances and if you are having trouble thinking of any, ask God to give you more opportunities to be blessed by your giving and kindness. Remember we sow what we reap so perhaps it wasn't a financial reward, maybe it was a word of encouragement you really needed, maybe it was in your health or the health of a loved one, maybe that family member you'd been praying for finally came to the Lord. You know your story better than anyone else, so don't forget to give God His glory for coming through on His promise to bless and prosper those who give earnestly.

So when you are debating whether or not to show kindness or give to those who are in need, look back on these verses as well as on what you've learned through this book. Maybe it will encourage you to act.

The Best Benefit Of Hospitality!

IN MY OPINION, THE best benefit of hospitality is that it makes us more like Christ. Isn't that the point of all this, anyhow? We are striving to be like Christ and the more you show kindness, mercy and compassion to those around you the more you become a good representative of Him on Earth.

For further proof, let's look at Matthew 8:1-4. In this passage, Jesus heals a leper, a man who had absolutely no business being in a crowd of people. He was shunned, sick and probably quite lonely. And yet, Jesus not only talked to this man but He touched the leper. Doing so would have made him ceremoniously "unclean." It was something that just wasn't done. EVER. And yet Jesus didn't question it or have to think about it. He allowed the man to approach, listened to the request, and did something about it.

And let us not forget Zacchaeus (Luke 19:1-10). He was shunned by his own people because he was a tax collector for the Romans, and a corrupt one at that. However, Jesus did not let the man's past misdeeds and even his current lifestyle be a wall that separated them. Jesus called up to the man watching him from a tree and dined with him. And thanks to the kindness of our Lord and Savior Jesus Christ, not only did Zacchaeus have a change of heart, but he then gave back four times what he had stolen from the people. When we are kind to others, we can cause a positive change that creates a domino effect. Jesus knew this and we ought to strive to be more like Him. Jesus' kindness stemmed from His love for people and as we begin to show kindness and compassion, we are stretching our hearts, building up our love.

Moreover, the more we follow after Christ, the closer we get to the Father. We should all want a closer relationship with Him and we can strengthen our relationship by doing what He has called us to do. After awhile, it will become second nature to us and we will get closer and closer to the Father the more we do it. What does this mean? It means we will be able to hear His voice clearer, we will be able to recognize when the Holy Spirit is leading us, we will be a better witness to those around us, and that we are adding jewels to our crowns of righteousness. (We will all wear a crown but the number of jewels you have depends on how you live this current life [2 Timothy 4:8].) I can't claim to know what you want, but when I receive my crown I want it to be full of jewels indicating that I lived a life of purpose and a life that was a good reflection of my Savior.

So, I say all that to say this: don't be stingy with your compassion, kindness and giving. Not only does it bless that other person, but it blesses you!

Don't miss out!

Visit the website below and you can sign up to receive emails whenever Chyina Powell publishes a new book. There's no charge and no obligation.

https://books2read.com/r/B-A-DLRN-IRYSC

BOOKS 2 READ

Connecting independent readers to independent writers.

About the Author

Chyina Powell is a freelance editor at Powell Editorial. She is also the founder of the nonprofit organization the Women of Color Writers' Circle that offers a safe space and community for women of color who write across the globe.

In her free time, Chyina can often be found with a book, a blanket and a hot cup of tea in her hands.

Read more at https://www.powelleditorial.org.